CHINESE ZODIAC
COLORING BOOK
MARY LOU BROWN & SANDY MAHONY

Copyright ©2016 Mary Lou Brown & Sandy Mahony
All rights reserved. No part of this book may be reproduced in any form or by any electronic or mechanical means including information storage and retrieval systems, without permission in writing from the authors. The only exception is by a reviewer, who may quote short excerpts in a review.

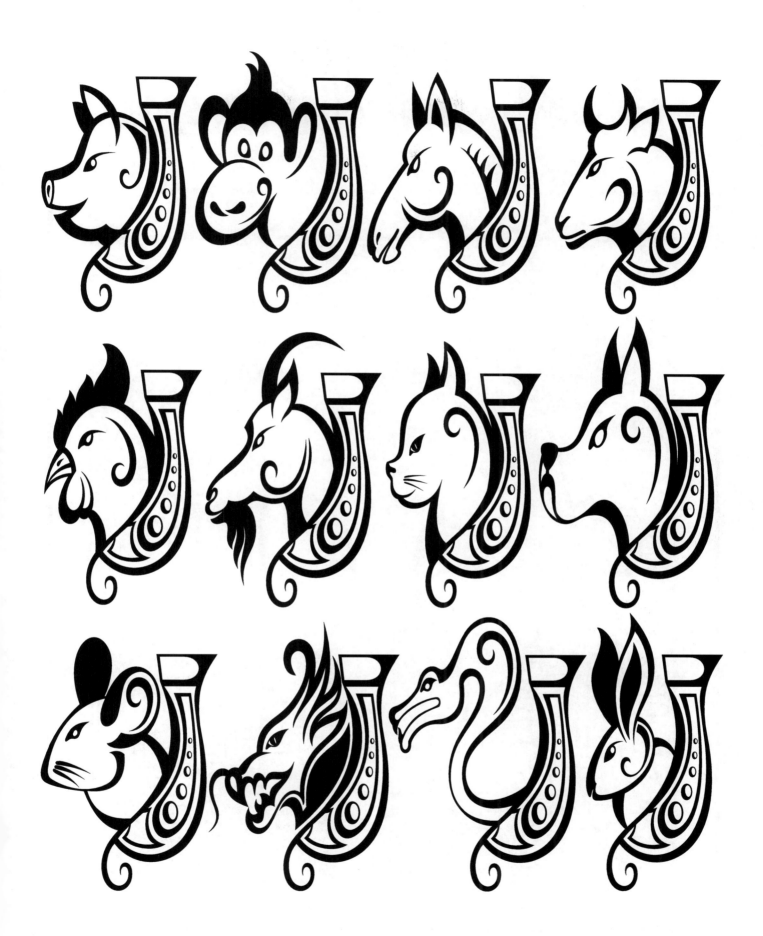

MONKEY

ROOSTER

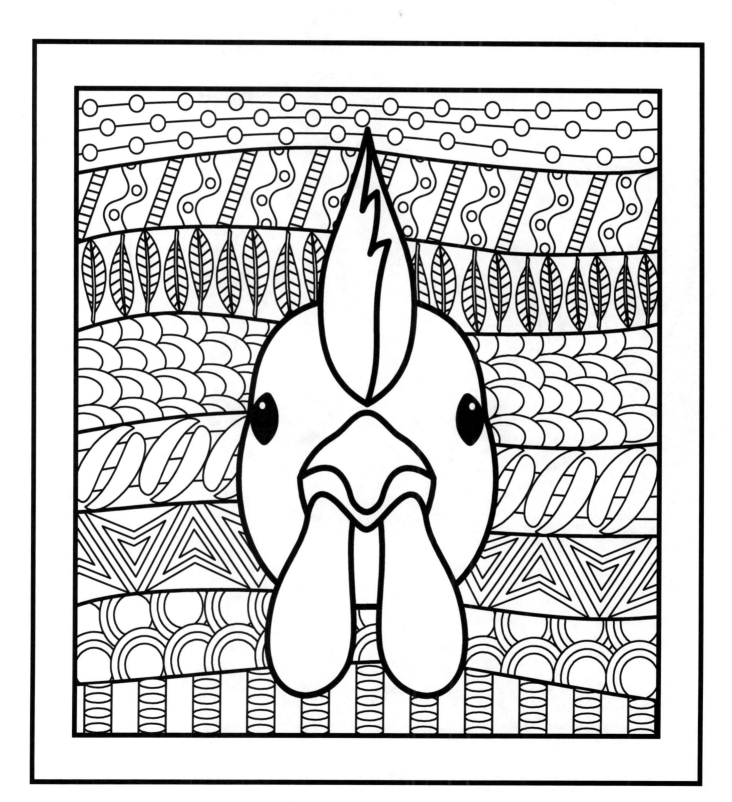

DOG

PIG

RAT

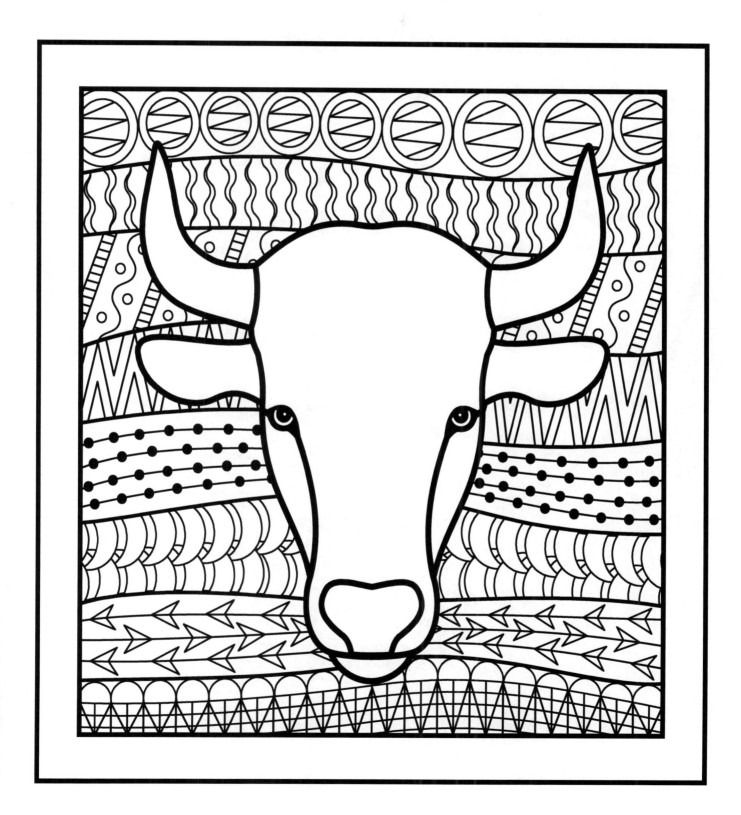

TIGER

RABBIT

DRAGON

SNAKE

HORSE

GOAT/SHEEP

Made in the USA
San Bernardino, CA
16 January 2017